PEAK DISTRICT PLACE NAMES

by Martin Spray

Maps by John N. Merrill

a J.N.M. PUBLICATION

1989

D1470854

a J.N.M. PUBLICATION

JNM PUBLICATIONS,
WINSTER,
MATLOCK,
DERBYSHIRE.
DE4 2DQ

This book is copyright under the Berne Convention. All rights are reserved. Apart from any fair dealing for the purposes of private study, research, criticism or review, as permitted under the Copyright Act, 1956, no part of this publication may be reproduced, stored in a retrieval system, or transmitted in any other form by any means, electronic, electrical, chemical, mechanical, optical, photocopying, recording or otherwise, without the prior permission of the copyright owner. Enquiries should be addressed to the publishers.

Typeset, designed, marketed and distributed by John N. Merrill.

© Text — Martin Spray 1989.

© Maps — John N. Merrill 1989

First Published — April 1989.

ISBN 0 907496 82 2

Meticulous research has been undertaken to ensure that this publication is highly accurate at the time of going to press. The publishers, however, cannot be held responsible for alterations, errors or omissions, but they would welcome notification of such for future editions.

Printed by: W. Hobson & Son Ltd., Northwich, Cheshire.

Set in Garamond, bold and italic.

ABOUT MARTIN SPRAY -

Martin Spray was born in Sheffield, and still likes to think he has some roots there and in the peat bogs, woods and dales of the Peak District. A botany graduate, he has been teaching students of landscape design for several years, and lives in the Forest of Dean — where he finds people almost as friendly as 'back home'. He is married to a landscape designer, and has two exhaustingly energetic young daughters.

He has written extensively on natural history, conservation, landscape and environmental education topics, and currently edits the magazine ECOS — A REVIEW OF CONSERVATION. His interest in place-names is a recurrent and very amateur hobby. More persistent interests include natural history, gardening and rambling — for all of which, as well as a love of the Peak District, he thanks his parents.

CONTENTS

INTRODUCTION

This booklet is not a scholarly treatise on local place names. My interest in names is entirely dilettante. But names are fascinating, and I hope that I can show something of their interest.

After a very short ramble through some of the background to place names in general, and Peak District names in particular, a series of maps shows present-day names in the region and suggested "translations" of them. These and other names can be explored more fully by using the Name Lists, and the Glossary which explains the (supposed) meanings of the original words that make up the names.

In order to produce these lists, I have relied very heavily upon the relevant county volumes published by the English Place-Name Society, supplemented by other sources. These, and other books and papers listed at the end of this booklet, are available in several local libraries.

There is still much to be discovered about place names (and, for that matter, family names) everywhere; and there are ample opportunities for exploring beyond the ones discussed here. Names studies make fascinating projects ; and with this in mind, a few suggestions for place name studies in schools are offered. I would be delighted to hear from teachers (or anyone else) who takes them up.

This booklet grew out of an attempt to gather some local names information together for the Peak Park Study Centre at Losehill (Pigsty Hill) Hall.

ABOUT PLACE NAMES...

Where
man has not been
to give
them names
objects
on desert islands
do not
know what they are.
Taking no chances
they stand still
and wait
quietly excited
for hundreds
of
thousands of
years.

Names do not excite everyone. Nonetheless, everyone uses them; and learning a district's many place names is an important task throughout life. In fact, most of us actually coin names for particular places that are of some significance to us — although they may not be significant to others, and such names may be very short-lived.

The first thing to remember about names, as Ivor Cutler hints in his poem 'What?', but the thing most often forgotten, is that they all mean something. They tell us what a thing is.

Often, however, they tell us the wrong thing: for example, I am (unwittingly) named after a Christian saint who is himself (probably unwillingly) named for the Roman God of War. The second thing to remember about names — place names and personal names, and indeed a lot of "household words" — is that over time they become redundant or meaningless, as the reasons behind them are forgotten or become irrelevant. Nobody seems sure what my surname means — although it may have developed from a Devon river name.

Take a couple of local examples. (Further details of the names discussed here are to be found in the Word List and Glossary sections.) What could be more obvious that Wildboarclough? — the ravine where wild boar were found. There have been no wild pigs here for quite a while; but at least the meaning is still clear. Less clear is Whatstandwell. Now, Walter Stonewell died in the late 14th Century, yet the place still bears his name. And what about contradictory Highlow? A hlaw, to the early "English" settlers, was a hill, and this particular one was noticeably higher than others nearby...

These three examples will serve to introduce the range of sources of names — and the reasons for giving places names. We give places names —- and are still doing it, of course, in several ways: perhaps because they are associated with particular people, or good hunting, poor soil, or some other physical characteristic. Highlow is topographic; it identifies a geographical feature. For obvious reasons, there are many such names in the Peak District — itself a topographic name.

Many other names are descriptive of a site's vegetation or some distinctive animal life there. Wildboarclough is an example of the latter. Cressbrook is a self-explanatory instance of the former. Trees, naturally, as much of the area was wooded when the Germanic and Scandinavian people settled here, feature prominently in Peak names. An interesting pair is One Ash and Monyash. A name such as Moscar spans both topographic and vegetational categories: a mos (present-day largely dialect "moss") is a bog or swamp, which has a very distinctive appearance, and kjarr (present-day semi-technical "carr") is wet ground overgrown with bushes.

When a phase of colonisation occurs, such as when the "English" moved into Celtic Britain — to them the British were Welsh (welisc, i.e. "foreigners"!) — settlement and habitation names are common. Some of these are rather bald; like Thorpe, which means an outlying farmstead or "daughter" settlement from an established village. Others tell a little of the conditions that were met by these "pioneers": Rowsley is the woodland clearing occupied, or perhaps made, by (Norse) Hrolfr or (English) Hrothwulf; Chatsworth is (English) Ceatt's enclosure.

These last two names are also examples of places named from persons. Just as many people are named after the places they or their ancestors inhabited (Derby-, Darbyshire is a frequent surname, for example: indeed, about half our surnames are derived from names of places), many settlements are named from their pioneers. We have already met another, rather different, example of a place taking over a person's name: Whatstandwell, first recorded in the name of a bridge near Walt's home — and Walt's family name, perhaps originally a nickname, is presumably taken from the characteristics of a local well. People are commemorated in names in another way. People give their names not only to countries, but also to smaller areas. Wales in South Yorkshire (and Wales names elsewhere — including the country) is where an enclave of "foreigners" lived.

Some places are named after occupations rather than personal names. A well-known one in the Peak is Jagger's Clough, which takes its title from the local lead carriers — the "jaggers".

Those personal names which are scattered around our landscapes have a number of origins. Indeed, our place names as a whole show a rough sequence of namers or sources, from some which are probably now inexplicable to the many new names that are still constantly being invented. Most up-to-date ones are relatively very minor, of course, and often of the fairly meaningless <u>Costa Fortune</u> type. Historically recent names of larger significance in the Peak include <u>New Mills</u>, a designation which has displaced the older name Middle Cale. The Norman takeover brought in a liberal scatter of old French elements and personal names, exemplified here by <u>Belper</u>, and the — en le — connections as in <u>Alsop en le Dale</u> and <u>Chapel en le Frith</u> — known to most modern locals as "<u>Chapel</u>" and to some as "Chapel Enli".

Most of our place names date back to the Old English period — roughly what used to be called Anglo-Saxon — when Germanic peoples settled here. In the North of England especially, they were followed by Scandinavian settlers, whose influence is still seen and heard. <u>Lathkill</u>, for example, consists of two Norse words; and several Scandinavian pioneers are commemorated locally. The Peak was within the Danelaw.

When the Germanic peoples colonised the country, Britain was already settled — by Celts, and probably also still by some pre-Celtic peoples. Some places named before the "English" phase still bear remnants of their ancient (but perhaps not oldest...) names. Many are obscure, difficult for experts to interpret, and hidden in subsequent English refashionings. <u>Parwich</u> seems to retain a British word for "bright" (water) wedded to an Old English term for, in this case probably, a dairy-farm. <u>Cheadle</u> is an interesting case, exemplifying a number around the country, where later settlers have added a word to "explain" the Celtic one: the name seems to translate as "Wood wood"!

However, it is the <u>river names</u> which show the pre-Germanic influence most forcefully. It has long been understood that in a largely forested landscape, rivers and major hills are likely to receive names early, and to retain these early names over long periods. The area's major river, the <u>Derwent</u>, like the Cumbrian and Northumbrian Derwents, and the Darwen and Dart, is "where oaks are abundant". It is perhaps disappointing, though, that so many ancient river names are thought to have more or less the simple meaning "water"...

The Peak District demonstrates quite a few repetitive names resulting from people forgetting earlier meanings. <u>Longdendale</u>, <u>Howden Clough</u>, and delightful <u>Alsop en le Dale</u> all "explain" Old English words for valleys. Once basic meanings have been lost, all manner of strange things can happen to place names. Some can, as it were, shrink, or enlarge: a classic case of the latter development is that enormous country called Canada — probably an Iroquois word for a small cabin, it was first noted by European settlers as the name of an Indian village! There seem not to be such blatant examples hereabouts, although one might look at the relative enormity of <u>Bradfield</u> township, or note how town and city names must spread as their administrative and physical boundaries expand. A clear example of enlargement is currently being shown by <u>Kinder Scout</u>, where the promontary name has for many people come to denote the whole plateau.

On the other hand, there are shrinkages. An interesting example — although also perhaps an example of "fragmentation" — is that of Lyme Forest, which once covered parts of at least four counties but which now no longer exists as an entity, but remains in localised names as at <u>Lyme Hall</u> and <u>Park</u>, <u>Ashton-under-Lyme</u>, and <u>Ilam</u>. It is curious to find the name <u>Peak Forest</u> attached to a small village (as the parish name), when initially it referred to the extensive mediaeval hunting area: a "forest" here does not mean woodland. The <u>Peak</u> District itself has shrunk in area since we first meet it as <u>Peac lond</u> in AD 924. Unfortunately, we are still unsure just what 'peak' referred to.

Some names don't so much shrink as disappear. Middle Cale was dispelled by up-and-coming <u>New Mill</u>(s). <u>Derby</u> itself is an interesting case. The first reference to the name appears as "in locum qui Northworthige nuncupatur juxta autem Danaam linguam Deoraby" — that is, what had been called North Enclosure by the Saxons was The Deer Farm to the Danes.

Other names move. The location of a name on a map or on signposts on the ground is no guarantee that this is the place originally meant. The several <u>Hope</u> names in the area mean a side-valley branching from a larger one, or a small enclosed valley. This does not describe what we now know as the Hope Valley; but it does describe Edale Vale, and the original settlement of Hope is in this branch.

Place names provoke some intriguing attempts at explanation — and not all of them are so-called folk etymology. There is a curious example near Hope. <u>Win Hill</u>, the story goes, was where the army of the Saxon king of Northumbria camped, before a battle. The unfortunate army of Wessex was, naturally, camped on <u>Lose Hill</u>...! Some events are rather better than legend. We are invited to call the top of Win Hill <u>Ward's Piece</u>, in memory of Sheffield walkers' champion G.H.B. Ward. The "meaning" behind this commemoration may already be lost except to devotees; and this relatively new name may, like very many place names, disappear after it ceases to be novel.

When the original meaning is lost, and no subsequent "explanation" is available, there is often little guidance as to how to say a name — especially when it is met in written form; and, indeed, many spellings have changed marvellously for the same reason. Take <u>Wightwizzle</u> near Broomhead. "Wite-wizzle" or "Wig-twizzle"?... It means "Wicga's piece of land at the stream junction" (<u>twisla</u>); so the occasional outsider's guess at "Wite-wizzle" is mistaken. So, in a way, is "Chapel Enli".

But this begs several questions, including: Who uses particular names?

and Who is responsible for names? There are obvious advantages if everyone uses the same name for a place; but there are too many names for us all to use. North of the junction with the River Westend and Ronksley Moor in the upper <u>Derwent Valley</u> is a small case of name preservation. The whole of the river from Featherbed Moss southwards is "officially" the Derwent; yet some locals and walkers retain a separate name for the moorland headwaters: <u>Ronksley River</u>, also wrongly (?) spelled "Wrongsley". Such a localised name is as useful to people familiar with the area as are street names to a city neighbourhood. Indeed, local communities needed, and still use, many more names than ever a visitor's map shows. Farming communities traditionally named all their fields. Most <u>field names</u> are neglected now, although preserved in deeds, old maps — and city street and district names. Peak District field names can be as bald (<u>Wheat Field</u>, <u>Far Field</u>), descriptive (<u>Top o' th' Bank</u>), <u>Bellond Field</u> — i.e. poisoned by lead), or poetic (<u>Brandy Bottle</u> — perhaps from its shape, <u>Bawdy Croft</u>, <u>Treacle Nook</u> — with sticky soil) as any in the country.

This is too fine detail for the following maps. Some more imortant places have also been left off the maps, simply because there are no satisfactory explanations of them — in some cases not even expert guesses. In fact, many place name interpretations are sensible guesses. The maps and alphabetical listings contain quite a few. In several cases the precise meanings suggested by researchers have not been used, but the attempt has been made to keep the <u>sense</u> of a name in a short form on the map, and to spell out the interpreation(s) in full in the list, the root-elements of the names being detailed in the glossary. Even this has left several cumbersome descriptions on the maps.

Any place-name expert who has read this far will have confirmed that this is not an especially erudite explanation of either the subject in general or Peak District names in particular. In preparing the accompanying maps, list and glossary, explanations have been drawn very largely from the English Place-Name Society volumes, especially those for Derbyshire and Yorkshire, and the <u>Concise Oxford Dictionary of English Place-Names</u> has been used as a first check because of the many alternatives it offers. Details of these and other useful books and articles are given after the Glossary at the end of the book.

There are numerous traps and pit-falls for the amateur student of place-names — and names generally — and I do not doubt that in trying to show something of their fascination I have caught myself!

Names, as we have seen, originate in a number of ways. Sometimes they have very small, apparently trivial origins, as this poetic example demonstrates:-

Women he liked, did shovel-bearded Bob,
Old Farmer Hayward of the Heath, but he
Loved horses. He himself was like a cob,

6

And leather-coloured. Also he loved a tree.
For the life in them he loved most living things,
But a tree chiefly. All along the lane
He planted elms where now the stormcock sings
That travellers hear from the slow-climbing train.
Till then the track had never had a name
For all its thicket and the nightingales
That should have earned it. No one was to blame.
To name a thing beloved man sometimes fails.
Many years since, Bob Hayward died, and now
None passes there because the mist and the rain
Out of the elms have turned the lane to slough
And gloom; the name alone survives, Bob's Lane.

(Edward Thomas, 'Women he loved')

THE MAPS

As explained in the Introduction, some major names are not represented on these maps, because we are so unsure why they are called what they are. Most other omissions are for the sake of clarity.

Names have been chosen to give a fairly wide cover, and to try to demonstrate a wide range of types of names. They also cover a fairly wide time span: that is, it must be remembered that not only the names but also settlements have appeared at different times over at least a couple of millennia. Even so, the oldest names represented are only the oldest names of those places <u>known to us</u>. Virtually all original acts of naming are beyond recall.

The National Park boundary is shown on the maps. Today's name is in italic letters and the meaning underneath is in bold.

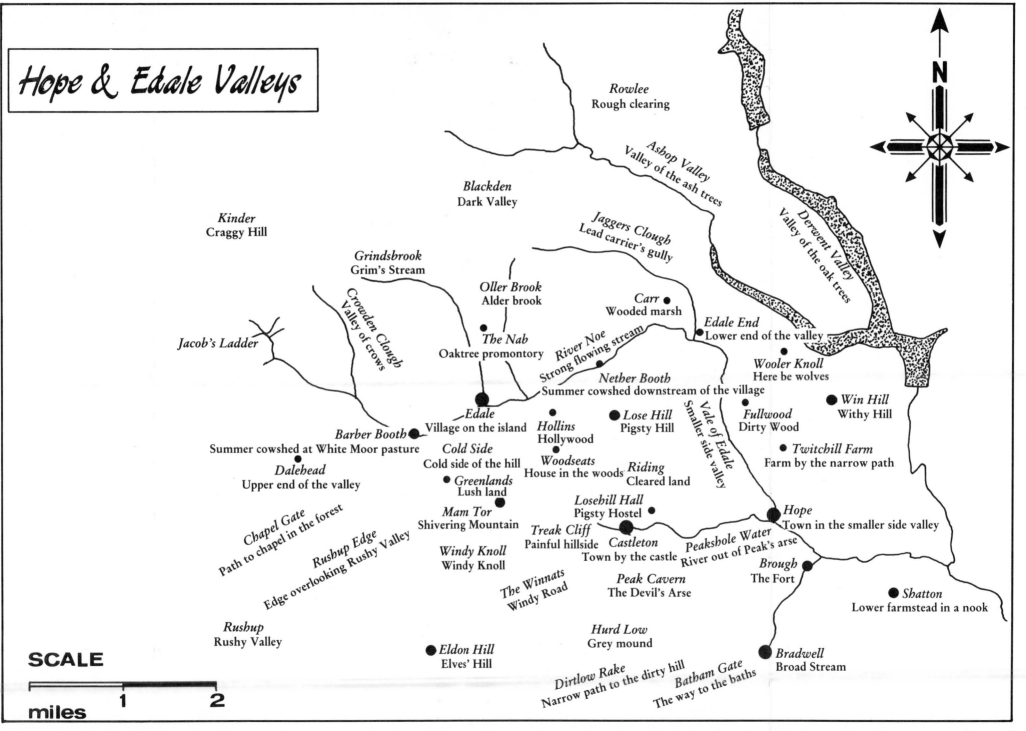

Hope & Edale Valleys

Rowlee
Rough clearing

Ashop Valley
Valley of the ash trees

Derwent Valley
Valley of the oak trees

Blackden
Dark Valley

Jaggers Clough
Lead carrier's gully

Kinder
Craggy Hill

Grindsbrook
Grim's Stream

Oller Brook
Alder brook

Carr
Wooded marsh

Crowden Clough
Valley of crows

Edale End
Lower end of the valley

Jacob's Ladder

River Noe
Strong flowing stream

The Nab
Oaktree promontory

Wooler Knoll
Here be wolves

Nether Booth
Summer cowshed downstream of the village

Edale
Village on the island

Win Hill
Withy Hill

Barber Booth
Summer cowshed at White Moor pasture

Hollins
Hollywood

Lose Hill
Pigsty Hill

Fullwood
Dirty Wood

Vale of Edale
Smaller side valley

Cold Side
Cold side of the hill

Woodseats
House in the woods

Riding
Cleared land

Twitchill Farm
Farm by the narrow path

Dalehead
Upper end of the valley

Greenlands
Lush land

Losehill Hall
Pigsty Hostel

Chapel Gate
Path to chapel in the forest

Mam Tor
Shivering Mountain

Hope
Town in the smaller side valley

Rushup Edge
Edge overlooking Rushy Valley

Treak Cliff
Painful hillside

Castleton
Town by the castle

Peakshole Water
River out of Peak's arse

Brough
The Fort

Windy Knoll
Windy Knoll

Peak Cavern
The Devil's Arse

Shatton
Lower farmstead in a nook

Rushup
Rushy Valley

The Winnats
Windy Road

Hurd Low
Grey mound

Eldon Hill
Elves' Hill

Dirtlow Rake
Narrow path to the dirty hill

Batham Gate
The way to the baths

Bradwell
Broad Stream

SCALE

miles   1   2

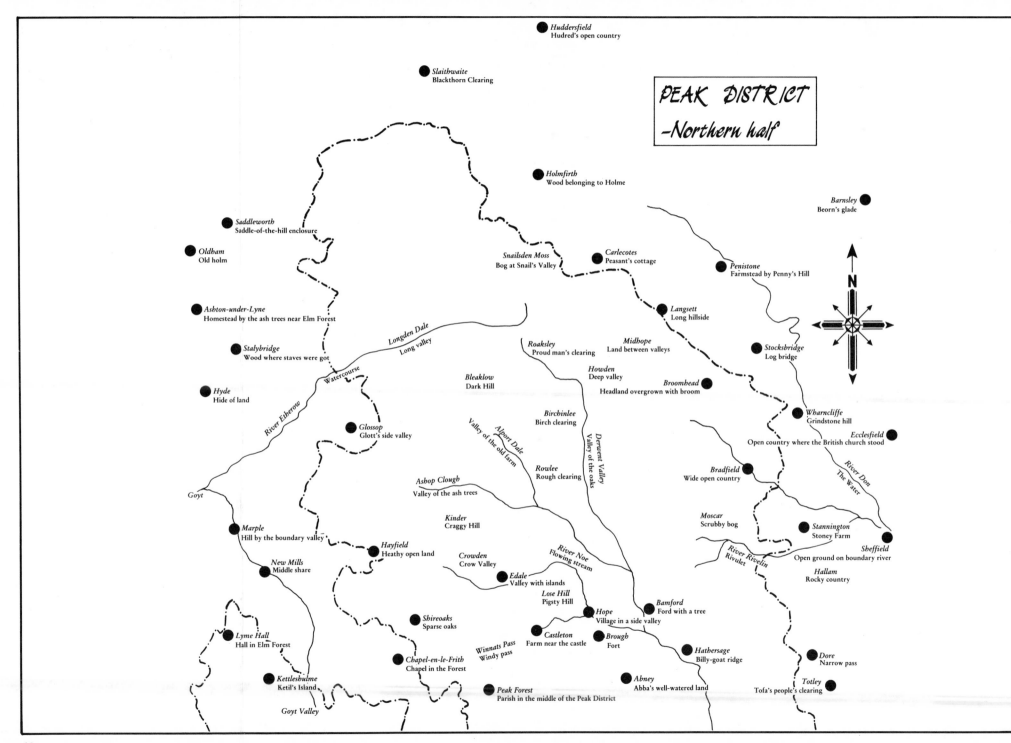

PEAK DISTRICT
–Northern half

Huddersfield — Hudred's open country

Slaithwaite — Blackthorn Clearing

Holmfirth — Wood belonging to Holme

Barnsley — Beorn's glade

Saddleworth — Saddle-of-the-hill enclosure

Oldham — Old holm

Snailsden Moss — Bog at Snail's Valley

Carlecotes — Peasant's cottage

Penistone — Farmstead by Penny's Hill

Ashton-under-Lyne — Homestead by the ash trees near Elm Forest

Langsett — Long hillside

Stalybridge — Wood where staves were got

Longden Dale — Long valley

Roaksley — Proud man's clearing

Midhope — Land between valleys

Stocksbridge — Log bridge

Hyde — Hide of land

Watercourse

Bleaklow — Dark Hill

Howden — Deep valley

Broomhead — Headland overgrown with broom

River Etherow

Birchinlee — Birch clearing

Wharncliffe — Grindstone hill

Glossop — Glott's side valley

Alport Dale — Valley of the old farm

Ecclesfield — Open country where the British church stood

Derwent Valley — Valley of the oaks

Rowlee — Rough clearing

Bradfield — Wide open country

River Don — The Water

Ashop Clough — Valley of the ash trees

Goyt

Kinder — Craggy Hill

Moscar — Scrubby bog

Stannington — Stoney Farm

Marple — Hill by the boundary valley

Hayfield — Heathy open land

Crowden — Crow Valley

River Noe — Flowing stream

River Rivelin — Rivulet

Sheffield — Open ground on boundary river

New Mills — Middle share

Edale — Valley with islands

Hallam — Rocky country

Lose Hill — Pigsty Hill

Bamford — Ford with a tree

Lyme Hall — Hall in Elm Forest

Shireoaks — Sparse oaks

Hope — Village in a side valley

Castleton — Farm near the castle

Brough — Fort

Hathersage — Billy-goat ridge

Dore — Narrow pass

Chapel-en-le-Frith — Chapel in the Forest

Winnats Pass — Windy pass

Abney — Abba's well-watered land

Totley — Tofa's people's clearing

Kettleshulme — Ketil's Island

Peak Forest — Parish in the middle of the Peak District

Goyt Valley

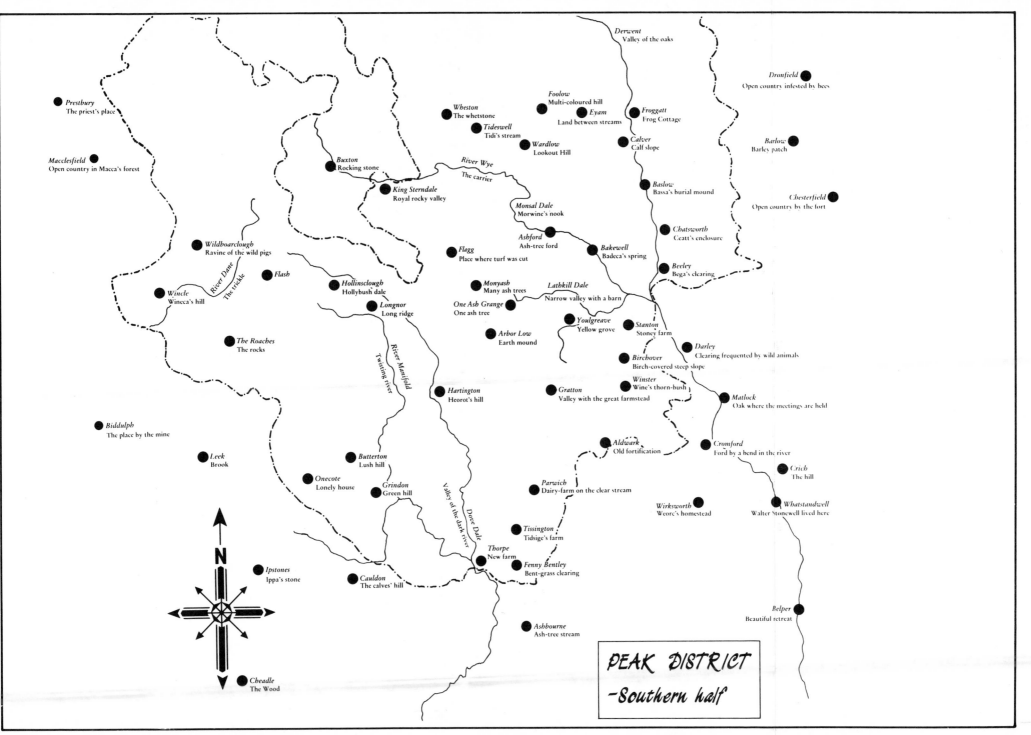

Derwent
Valley of the oaks

Dronfield
Open country infested by bees

Foolow
Multi-coloured hill

Wheston
The whetstone

Eyam
Land between streams

Froggatt
Frog Cottage

Tideswell
Tidi's stream

Wardlow
Lookout Hill

Calver
Calf slope

Barlow
Barley patch

Prestbury
The priest's place

Macclesfield
Open country in Macca's forest

Buxton
Rocking stone

River Wye
The carrier

Baslow
Bassa's burial mound

Chesterfield
Open country by the fort

King Sterndale
Royal rocky valley

Monsal Dale
Morwine's nook

Chatsworth
Ceatt's enclosure

Wildboarclough
Ravine of the wild pigs

Ashford
Ash-tree ford

Bakewell
Badeca's spring

Beeley
Bega's clearing

Flagg
Place where turf was cut

Wincle
Wineca's hill

Flash

River Dane
The trickle

Hollinsclough
Hollybush dale

Monyash
Many ash trees

Lathkill Dale
Narrow valley with a barn

Longnor
Long ridge

One Ash Grange
One ash tree

Youlgreave
Yellow grove

Stanton
Stoney farm

Darley
Clearing frequented by wild animals

The Roaches
The rocks

Arbor Low
Earth mound

River Manifold
Twisting river

Birchover
Birch-covered steep slope

Winster
Wine's thorn-bush

Hartington
Heorot's hill

Gratton
Valley with the great farmstead

Matlock
Oak where the meetings are held

Biddulph
The place by the mine

Aldwark
Old fortification

Cromford
Ford by a bend in the river

Leek
Brook

Butterton
Lush hill

Crich
The hill

Onecote
Lonely house

Grindon
Green hill

Parwich
Dairy-farm on the clear stream

Wirksworth
Weorc's homestead

Whatstandwell
Walter Stonewell lived here

Valley of the dark river

Dove Dale

Tissington
Tidsige's farm

Ipstones
Ippa's stone

Thorpe
New farm

Fenny Bentley
Bent-grass clearing

Cauldon
The calves' hill

N

Belper
Beautiful retreat

Cheadle
The Wood

Ashbourne
Ash-tree stream

PEAK DISTRICT
-Southern half

NAME LIST

THE NAMES on all the maps are included in this list.

The entries show:-
- an explanation of the name, often fuller or more literal than appears on the map;
- the name elements, which are explained in the Glossary;
- the form of the first recording of the name, and its date (sometimes only to a period); DB is Domesday Book of 1086;
- significant changes in the name are indicated, with their first recorded form and date;
- in some cases an explanatory note is added.

Abney	"Abba's well-watered land" personal name, e.g. Habenai DB.
Aldwark	"Old fortification" ald, weorc. Ald(e)werk(e) &c. c.1140.
Alport	"Old town" ald, port. Aldeport 1285.
Alsop en le Dale	"ælli's valley" personal name, hop, (OFr en le, dæl). Elleshope DB.
Arbor Low	"Earth-work mound" eorth-burg, hlaw. Harberlowe 1533.
Ashbourne	"Ash-tree stream" (now called Henmore Brook) æsc, burna. Esse-, Eseburn(e), -burna, &c DB.
Ashford	"Ash-tree ford" æsc, ford. (at) æscforda 926 (recorded C13).
Ashop Clough	"Ash-tree valley" æsc, hop (cloh). Essop(e), -opp, hop(e) reign of John.
Ashton-Under-Lyne	"Homestead by the ash-trees" æsc, tun. Eston 1212. Asshton under Lyme 1305-. See Lyme Hall.

Bakewell

"B(e)adeca's spring"
personal name, <u>wælla</u>. (to) Bedecan wiellon
924.

Bamford

"Ford with a tree (perhaps as a footbridge)"
<u>beam</u>, <u>ford</u>. Banford DB.

Barber Booth

formerly Whitemorley Booth, "Summer
cowshed (or shelter) at white moor pasture"
<u>hwit</u>, <u>mor</u>, <u>leah</u>, (later <u>both</u>). Whitmoreley
1579. Barber Booth 1675, from local family
name. There were several other booths in the
area.

Barlow Either

"Boar clearing" or "Clearing where
barley grew"
<u>bar</u> or <u>bær</u>, <u>leah</u>. Barleie DB.

Barnsley

"Beorn's clearing or glade"
personal name, <u>leah</u>. Berneslai DB.

Baslow

"Bassa's burial-mound"
personal name, <u>hlaw</u>.
Basselau DB.

Batham Gate

"The way to the Baths"
<u>bæth</u>, <u>gata</u>. Bathinegate (for Bathmegate)
1400. Roman road from Brough to Buxton.

Beeley

"Bega's clearing"
personal name, <u>leah</u>. Begelei DB.

Belper

"Beautiful retreat"
<u>beau</u>, <u>repaire</u>. Be(a)urepeir, -repeyr, &c
1231-.

Biddulph

? "The place by the mine"
? <u>bi</u>, <u>delfan</u>. Bidolf DB.

Birchinlee

"Forest clearing with birches"
<u>birce</u>, <u>leah</u>. Birchynley(e), Birchine- 1285.

Birchover

"Birch-covered steep slope"
<u>birce</u>, <u>ofer</u>. Barcovere DB.

Blackden

"Dark valley"
<u>blæc</u>, <u>denu</u>. Blackden End 1627.

Bleaklow

"Dark hill"
<u>blæc</u>, <u>hlaw</u>. Blacke lowe 1617.

Bradfield	"Wide stretch of open country" brad, feld. Bradesfeld 1188.
Bradwell	"The broad stream" brad, wælla. Bradewell(e), -wella DB.
Broomhead	"Headland overgrown with broom" (but see glossary) brom, heafod. Bromyheued 1280.
Brough	"Fort" (Roman Navio) burh. Burc 1195.
Butterton	"Butter hill", i.e. "Hill with lush pasture" butere, dun. Buterdon 1200.
Buxton	? "Rocking stone" (or perhaps "Buck stone") bug-stan (or bucc, stan). Buchestanes 1108.
Calver	"Calf slope" calf, ofer. Calvoure DB.
Carlecotes	"Churl's cottage" karl (OE ceorl), cot. Carlecotes C13.
Carr (House)	"Wooded marsh" kjarr. The Carr in Edale 1699.
Castleton	"Farmstead near the castle" castel, tun. Castelton(e) C13 (First recorded as "uillata de Pecco" 1210.)
Cauldon	"Calves' hill" calf, dun. Celfdun 1002.
Chapel en le Frith	"Chapel in (Peak) Forest" chapel(e), fryhth, OFr en le. capellam de Frich' 1241. (First recorded as Ecclesia de Alto Peccho, "Church of the High Peak", 1219.)
Chapel Gate	"The way to Chapel en le Frith" chapel, gata.

Chatsworth	"Ceatt's enclosure" personal name, <u>worth</u>. Chetesuorde DB.
Cheadle	? "<u>Chet</u> wood"; i.e. "Wood wood" — an English word being added to explain a British one. ? <u>ceto</u>, <u>leah</u>. ? Cedde DB.
Chesterfield	"Open country near to or belonging to the fortification" <u>ceaster</u>, <u>feld</u>. Cestrefeld DB.
Coldside	"Cold (North) side of the hill" Cold Side 1840.
Crich	"The hill" <u>cruc</u>. Crice DB.
Cromford	"Ford by a bend in the river" <u>crumb</u>, <u>ford</u>. Crunforde DB.
Crowden Clough	"Crow valley" <u>crawe</u>, <u>denu</u>, (<u>cloh</u>). Crowden(e) 1550.
Dale Head	"Upper end of the valley" <u>dæl</u>, <u>heafod</u>. Dalehead 1627.
Dane, River	"Trickling stream" ? cf. <u>dafn</u>. Dauen c.1200.
Darley	"Clearing frequented by wild animals" <u>deor</u>, <u>leah</u>. Derelei(e) DB.
Derwent	"Abounding in oaks" from <u>derventju</u>. (in) Deorwentan 1009.
Dirtlow Rake	"Narrow path to dirty hill" <u>drit</u>, <u>hlaw</u>, (<u>rake</u>). Dyrtlo Rake hed 1538.
Don, River ?	"Water" <u>dana</u>. Don c.1200.
Dore	"Narrow pass" (on the Mercia-Northumbria border) <u>dor</u>. Dore 827.
Dove Dale	"Valley of the dark stream" (for the whole valley) <u>dubo-</u>, <u>dæl</u>. Duvesdale 1269.

Dronfield	"Open country infested with drones" d<u>ran</u>, <u>feld</u>. Dranefeld(e) DB.
Ecclesfield	"Open country in which a church of the British (i.e. Celts) stood" <u>eclesia</u>, <u>feld</u>. Eclesfelt DB.
Edale	"Valley with 'islands' of ground between streams" <u>eg</u>, <u>dæl</u>. Aidele DB.
Edale End	see Edale. Edall end 1659. (Edale-Hope boundary).
Eldon Hill	"Elves' hill" <u>elf</u>, <u>dun</u>, (<u>hyll</u>). Elvedon 1285. (Nearby Eldon Hole and tumuli probably prompted the name.)
Etherow, River	?"Watercourse-hill river" ?<u>edre</u>, <u>hoh</u>. Ederhou 1226.
Eyam probably	"Land between streams" <u>eg</u>. Aiune DB.
Fenny Bentley	"Bent-grass clearing" <u>beonet</u>, <u>leah</u>, (with later <u>fennig</u>). Benedlege DB. Fenni, -y bent(e)ley(e), -lee 1271.
Flagg	"Place where turves were cut" (for fuel perhaps) <u>flag</u>. Flagun DB.
Flash	"Swampy ground" <u>flasshe</u>.
Foolow probably	"Multi-coloured hill" <u>fag</u>, <u>hlaw</u>. Foulowe, Fow- 1269.
Froggatt probably	"Frog cottage" (because of low-lying riverside site) <u>frogga</u>, <u>cot</u>. Froggecot(e) 1225.
Fullwood	"Dirty wood" <u>ful</u>, <u>wudu</u>. Folwode 1497.
Glossop	"Glott's valley" personal name, <u>hop</u>. Glosop DB.

Goyt Valley	doubtful: "Watercourse" ?? <u>gota</u>. Guit 1244.
Greenlands	"Green land", perhaps from richness of grass here. Green Land 1670.
Grindon	"Green hill" <u>grene</u>, <u>dun</u>. Grendone DB.
Grindsbrook	"Grim's stream" personal (or Scandinavian god) name, <u>broc</u>. Grymesbrok(e) 1342.
Hallam ?	"Rocky country" ? <u>hall(r)</u>. Hallun DB. (Other explanations have been offered.)
Hartington	probably "Heorot's hill" personal name, <u>-ing-</u>, <u>dun</u>. Hortendun DB.
Hayfield	"Heathy open country" or "Open country where hay is got" <u>hæth</u>, <u>feld</u> or <u>heg</u>, <u>feld</u>. Hedfelt DB. (It has been suggested that two places are confused here.)
Hathersage	"He-goat ridge"; or ? "Haefer's ridge" <u>hæfer</u>, <u>ecg</u>; or personal name, <u>ecg</u>. Hereseige DB. Probably what is now called Millstone Edge.
Hollins	"Holly trees" <u>holegn</u> (later <u>hollin</u>). Hollins Cross 1688.
Hollinsclough	"Valley with holly-bushes" <u>holegn</u>, <u>cloh</u>.
Hollowford (Road)	"Ford in a hollow" <u>hol</u>, <u>ford</u>. le Holoforthe 1455.
Holmfirth	"Wood belonging to (place called) Holme" <u>holm</u>, <u>fyrhth</u>. (le) Holnefrith 1274-1324.
Hope	"Side valley" (perhaps originally that of the Noe) <u>hop</u>. (at) Hope 926 (recorded in C13).

Hope Valley	see above. Hope Valley must have been the side valley now called the Vale of Edale, not the main valley it now designates.
Howden Clough	"Deep valley" hol, denu, (cloh). Holden C14.
Huddersfield	"Hudraed's (or Huder's) piece of open country" personal name, feld. Oderesfelt DB.
Hurd Low	"Grey hill" har, hlaw. Horlowe 1327.
Hyde	"Hide (of land)" hid. Hyde 1285.
Ipstones	"Ippa's stone" personal name, stan. Yppestan 1175.
Jacob's Ladder	Commemorates the path cut by Jacob Marshall in the 18th Century.
Jaggers Clough	"Lead-carriers' gully" jagger (later cloh). Jagers Gate 1658; gata.
Kettlehulme	"Ketil's holm" personal name, holm. Keteleshulm 1285.
Kinder Scout	? "Craggy hill" Kinder is unexplained, but may be a British hill name. Chendre DB. skuti. Kinder Scout 1167. Kinder Scout must originally have been only one part of the plateau that now bears the name. "Craggy hill" is but poetic licence on my part!
King Sterndale ?	"Royal rocky valley" stæner, dæl. Stauredal(e), -dala 1101- 8; cyning. Kingus Stenerdale 1419.
Langsett	"Long hillside" (north side of Little Don valley) lang, side. Langeside, -syde C12.

Lathkill Dale	"Narrow valley with a barn" hlatha, kill (with later dæl). Lathegyll 1280.
Leek	"Brook" lec. Lec DB.
Longdondale	"Long valley" lang, denu (with later dæl). Langedenedele DB.
Longnor	"Long ridge or hillslope" lang, ofer. Langenoure 1227.
Lose Hill	"Pigsty hill" hlose, hyll. Looshill 1599.
Losehill Hall	"Pigsty hill Hall"; see above. Lousehill 1670.
Lyme (Hall)	"(Hall in) Elm Forest" ? from lemo. Lyme 1313. Lyme was a large area of forest in Cheshire-Lancashire-Staffordshire-Shropshire, including Macclesfield Forest.
Macclesfield perhaps	"Open country in Macca's Forest" (Mackley being a rather distant Derbyshire place) personal name, leah, feld. Maclesfeld DB.
Mam Tor also called	"Shivering or Shimmering Mountain" from frequent small falls of shale from steep face. Mam possibly a Celtic hill name. Manhill 1577; Mantaur 1630.
Manifold, River	"River with many folds" manig, falde. Manifold c. 1540. Ilam may derive from an older name for this river.
Marple	"Hill by the boundary valley" mær, hyll. Merpel 1248.
Matlock	probably "Oak where the meetings were held" mæthel, ac. Matlac, -ak 1204-; but DB has Meslach.

22

Midhope	"Land between valleys" (i.e. higher ground) or "Land in the middle of the valley" mid, hop. Middehop 1235.
Monsal Dale	"Morwine's nook" personal name, halh (with later dæl). Morleshal 1200.
Monyash	"Many ash-trees" manig, æsc. Maneis DB.
Moscar	"Scrubby bog; overgrown marsh" mos, kjarr. (Moscar Cross 1771)
The Nab	" (Oak-tree) projection (of hillside)" acen, nabbi. Oken Nabbe 1659.
Nether Booth	"Lower (below the village) summer cowshed" neothera, both. Nether bouth 1577. It became an alternative name for (Our) Lady Booth: "Lady Bowth otherwise Tunstydleyghe" 1554-8; hlæfdige, tun-stede. There were several other booths in the area.
New Mills	The original name perhaps meant "Middle share of land" — Middle Cale. middel, cavel. Midelcauel 1306. This is older name for town of New Mill (wrongly New Mills), from mill predating 1640.
Noe, River	"Flowing (stream)" ? nav-. Noue 1300.
Oldham	"Old holm" (see glossary) ald, holm. Aldholm 1226.
Ollerbrook	"Alder brook" alor, broc. Olerbroche 1561 (as name of the Booth).
One Ash (Grange)	"One ash-tree" an, æsc, (with later graunge). Aneise DB.
Onecotes	"Hut or cottage by itself" an, cot. Anecote 1199.

Parwich	? "Dairy-farm on the River Pever" (Ekwall assumes Pever to be the now unnamed stream running through the village) ? pebro, wic. Peuerwick 966 (recorded C13)
Peak Cavern	"Peak's arse" peac, ears. (Pechefers) Pechesers DB Locally known as "Devil's arse"; Devillsarse 1630. See Peakshole Water.
Peak Forest	"Forest of the Peak" peac, foresta. foresta de Pecco, Pecko 1223; (Peac lond 924). The name did, of course, apply to the whole region, only latterly to a parish; which peak(s) is unclear.
Peakshole Water	"Stream out of the Devil's arse"; see Peak Cavern. aquam de Pekisersse 1308. Peakshold River 1730.
Penistone	possibly "The farmstead by Penny's hill" ?? a nickname, tun. Pangeston, Pen- DB. There may have been a local hill-name derived from pening; or possibly from British penno- (cf. O Welsh penn: hill, height.
Peveril Castle	Land and castle held by William Peverel, son of William the Conqueror. Castelii de Pech 1173.
Prestbury	"The priest's manor or house" preost, burh. Presteburia c. 1175.
Riding (House)	"Land cleared of trees" rydding. Rydings 1547.
Rivelin	"Rivulet" riveling. Ri-, Ryvelyng, -ing C13.
The Roaches	"The rocks" roche.
Ronksley	"Ranc's clearing" ? nickname from ranc, leah. Rownkesley C15.

Rowlee	"Rough clearing" ruh, leah. Rowlee late C15.
Rushup	"Rushy valley" risc, hop. Rishop C13.
Rushup Edge	see above. Rushoppedge c.1620.
Saddleworth	"Saddle-ridge enclosure" sadol, worth. Sadelwrth C12.
Shatton	formerly Lower Shatton; "Farmstead in nook of land (between streams)" (neothera), sceat, tun. Scetune DB; Nethershatton 1508.
Sheffield	"Open country on Boundary River" sceath, feld. Scafeld DB.
Shireoaks	"Shining oak-trees" or "Area where oaks grow thinly" scir, ac. Shayrookes late C15.
Slaithwaite	"Blackthorn clearing" slah, thveit. Sladweit, -wait 1178.
Snailsden Moss	"Bog at Snail's valley" ? nickname, denu,(mos).
Spital Buildings	A mainly leper hospital founded by wife of William Peverel (see above) spitel. hospital de Castilton 1373; le Spyttell 1548.
Stalybridge	"Wood where staves were got": originally Staveley staef, leah. Stavel' 1285.
Stannington	probably "Stony farm" stan, -ing, tun. Stanygton C13.
Stanton in Peak	"Stony farm" stan, tun. Stantune DB. Staunton in Peake late C13.
Stocksbridge	"Bridge made of logs" stocc, brycg.

Thorpe	"(Outlying) farm" thorp.
Tideswell	"Tidi's stream" personal name, wælla. Ti-, Tydes-, -is-, -uswell(e) DB.
Tissington	"Tidsige's farm" personal name, -ing-, tun. Tizinctun DB.
Totley	"Wood or clearing of Tota's people" personal name, -inga-, leah. Totingelei DB.
Treak Cliff ?	"Painful hillside" ? trega, ac (later clif). Trayoc(k), Traiok 1285.
Twitchell (Farm)	"(Farm by the) narrow path" twicen(e). Twycell 1376.
Wardlow	"Lookout hill" weard, hlaw. Wardelowe 1258.
Wharncliffe	"Hillside where hand grindstones (querns) or millstones were made" cweorn, clif. Querncliffe 1406.
Whatstandwell	"Where Walter Stonewell lived" personal name: he signed himself Walt' Standewell (1347). Wattestanwell ford 1390
Wheston	"Whetstone" hwet-stan. Weston 1225.
Wildboarclough	"Ravine of the wild boar" wilde, bar, cloh.
Wincle	"Wineca's hill" personal name, hyll. Winchal C12.
Windy Knoll	(cnol). Windy Knowle 1771.
Win Hill	? "Hill where withies were got" withign, hyll. Wythinehull late C13.
Winnats	"Windswept pass" wind, geat. (le) Wyndegates 1330.

Winster	"Wine's thorn-bush" personal name, <u>thyrne.</u> Winsterne DB.
Wirksworth	"Weorc's or Wyrc's enclosure" personal name, <u>worth.</u> Wyrcesuuyrthe 835 (recorded C14)
Woodseats	"House in the woods" <u>wudu,</u> <u>sæte.</u> Woodseates 1594.
Wooler Knoll	"Wolves' hill" <u>wulf,</u> <u>hlaw</u> (later <u>cnol</u>). Wulwelauwe reign of Henry III.
Wye, River	possibly from Br. from Latin <u>vehere,</u> to carry; or perhaps pre-Celtic.
Youlgreave	"Yellow grove" or "Geola's grove" <u>geolu,</u> <u>græfe</u> or personal name, <u>græfe.</u> Giolgrave DB.

GLOSSARY

Most or the basic elements of the names shown on the maps and given in the above list are included here — a few others are either explained above, or are from names of relatively late date in which they have their modern meanings. In a few cases a note of explanation is added; but most of the
"definitions" are very brief. Anyone with access to a good dictionary (not necessarily of Old English) can find out much more about many of these words and their history, by working backwards!

The bar over some vowels(-) indicates that they are
"long" (bite rather than bit). Modern English 'th' is used rather than the Old English letters: see <u>thyrne</u>. <u>u</u> and <u>v</u> were seldom distinguished until late. <u>æ</u> was a vowel between a and e, usually rather like the 'a' in 'ash' which is its name.

OE is Old English ("Ango-Saxon") — up to about 1150. Unless marked otherwise, the words here are OE.

ME is Middle English — about 1150 to about 1450.

OD is Old Danish.

ON is Old Norse.

OFr is Old French.

Br is British — that is, one of the Celtic languages the Germanic colonists met in Britain.

W is Welsh.

ald	old
āc	oak; <u>ācen</u>, oaken, covered in oak-trees
æsc	ash-tree
alor	alder-tree
ān	one, single

bær	barley
baeth	bath(s)
bār	boar
bēam	tree, beam of timber
beau OFr	beautiful
beonet	bent-grass (Agrostis)
bi	by, beside
birce	birch; bircen abounding with birch-trees
blaec	dark, black
bōth OD bothe ME	booth, temporary shelter
brād	wide-open, broad
brōc	brook, stream
brōm	the rootword seems to signify "plant with prickles", and has derivatives meaning brambles as well as gorse or broom. Either of the last two would suit here, but broom is usually indicated in placenames.
brycg	bridge
bucc	buck
būg-stān	rocking-stone
burh, burg	fort, fortified place; later fortified house, house; later town, borough
burna	spring, stream
būtere	butter
cælf	calf
castel Br and Fr as well as OE	camp; castle

cavel ME	share (cf. dialect "Bide your cale" - Wait for your share; Wait your turn); allotment of land
ceaster	old fortification (not necessarily a castle); city
cēto- Br	wood (cf. W coed)
chapel OFr, ME	chapel
clif	steep bank or slope, cliff
clōh	clough, deep valley, dell
cnol(l)	summit, hilltop; later hillock, knoll
cot(e)	hut, cottage; also shelter for sheep
crāwe	crow
cruc Br	hill
crumb	bend of river
cweorn	quern (hand-operated grindstone for grain), millstone
cyning, cyng	king
dæl	dale, hollow
dafn W	a drop; dafnol, dropping, trickling. Also cf. Norwegian dave, a pool.
dānā (Celt) Br	water
delfan	dig — digging(s)
denu	valley (dene)
deor	animal; later deer
derventju- Br	? from root dervā (cf. W derwen) oak
dor	gate, door; entrance to a pass, a narrowing valley

drān	drone bee
drit OE, ON	dirt
dubo- Br	dark, black
dūn	hill (down, dune)
ears	buttock
eclēsia Br	church
ēdre	watercourse
ēg	island, dry ground in wet area or in river junction
elf	elf, fairy
eorth-burg	earth-work
fāg, fāh	coloured, multi-coloured
falde ME	fold (e.g. of river)
feld	open country (without trees); later field
fennig	dirty, muddy; marshy
flag ON	turf, sod
flasshe ME	pool, swamp, marshy grassland (flask OD)
ford	ford
foresta	forest; area reserved for hunting (not necessarily covered in trees)
frogga	frog
fūl, fuhl	dirty, foul
fyrhth	woodland, afforested ground (cf. W ffridd)
gata	way, path, road
gēat, gæt	opening, gap, gate(way)
geolu	yellow

gota Br	watercourse (? cf. W g<u>wyth</u>, channel, drain, vein (of blood))
graefe	copse, grove
graunge OFr grange ME	barn, granary; grange; outlying farm of a lord or monastery
grēne	green
halh	corner of land, nook
hall hallr ON	rock, boulder
hār	grey, hoar(y)
hēafod	head; headland
hīd	hide of land — a variable area: "enough to maintain a family"; "that which one plough can cultivate"
hlāefdige	lady; Our Lady
hlatha ON	barn
hlāw	hillock, hill, burial mound
hoh	projecting ridge of land
holegn	holly; ME <u>hollin</u>(g)
holm holmr ON	patch of dry land in marshy area; island in river; also watermeadow
hop	enclosed valley, small side valley
hwet-stān	whetstone
hwīt	white; also dry(pastureland)
hyll	hill, high ground
-ing-	linking element, as between personal name and topographic term

-inga-	element indicating (named) group
jagger	dialect "man in charge of jagging horses", i.e. which carried lead ore. Cf. Thomas le Jager 1308.
karl ON ceorl OE	churl, freeman, peasant
kill ON	narrow bay (of sea); narrow valley
kjarr ON ker ME	carr, marsh overgrown with bushes or trees
lang	long
lēah	wood; clearing in a wood (usually the latter here)
lec, lecc, laecc	brook
lemo, limo Celtic	elm; elmwood
maer	boundary
maethel	meeting, assembly
mam ?Br	perhaps a Celtic hill name; but the other predictable theory derives the word from Gaelic/Irish mamm, breast, or W mam, mother.
manig, monig	many
mid; middel	middle
mōr	waste(land), moor
mos, mosi ON	moss, i.e. bog, swampy ground
nabbi, nabbr ON	hill, knoll, projecting peak
nāv- Br	flow
neothera, nithera	lower, nether

ofer	(rising) hillslope, ridge
pēac	knoll, hill, peak
pebro- Br	? bright, radiant (cf. W pefr)
port	harbour; town, market.
prēost	priest
rake rakke ME	rough hill-path, narrow path (in ravine); probably from OE hraca, throat; narrow pass. Locally used in term lead rake, a surface vein.
ranc	proud, insolent
repaire OFr	place of retreat
risc	rush
riveling ME	rivulet, rill
roche OFr	rock
rūh	rough
rydding ME	clearing, land cleared of trees
sadol	saddle; saddle-shaped hill
sǣte	house; but possibly also set, dwelling, camp, animal fold
scēat	corner of land, nook
scēath	boundary
scīr	shining, bright; also thin(sheer), thinly grown, clear of weeds
side	side, hillside
skuti ON	projecting cliff, overhanging rock
slāh	sloe, blackthorn
spitel ME	hospital; a religious house

stæf	stave of wood, staff
stæner	stony, rocky ground
stān	stone, rock
stocc	treetrunk, stake
trega	affliction
tūn	originally fence, enclosure; early took on the meaning homestead, farmstead; and later, village, town
tūn-stēde	farmstead
twicen	narrow path
thorp OScand., OE	newly reclaimed site, new settlement, outlying farm
thveit ON thwēt OE	clearing; meadow, paddock
thyrne	thorn-bush; thorn (ϸyrne: the rune is ᚦ named after this word; the other Old Germanic letter for which we use 'th', ð is called 'edh' or 'eth'.)
wælla	spring, issue of water; well
weard	watch, ward, protection; later the administrative ward
weorc	work(s), structure, fortification
wīc	quarter of town, village; dwelling; farm — especially dairy farm
wilde	undomesticated, wild
wind	wind
withign	willow, willow woodland
worth	originally fence, enclosure; homestead
wudu	wood, woodland
wulf	wolf

A PLACE FOR NAMES IN SCHOOLS

There are several ways in which names in general, and place names in particular, can be brought into school work, at several levels.

If the interest inherent in names can be made use of, the meanings of the names themselves can provide an excellent means by which they can be learned. This could be a boost to local geography and history studies, and to environmental education. Specifically, some educational objectives of work with place names are:-

* to provide an opportunity for children to learn the various districts and "places" (their territory) that they ought to be familiar with;

* to investigate what we mean by a "place", what characterises it, and how it becomes named;

* to investigate the meanings and origins of these names;

* to provide material for local history and geography studies;

* to provide opportunities for word and language studies, and to see how words and language change.

It is often remarkably difficult to achieve a sense of historical perspective. Place names can introduce us to the landscapes and events of the past, and may even tell us not only what was done there but also that such people as Ippa, Beorna and Alf did it! This may lead into several kinds of study, including maps, settlement patterns and development, and into landscape and agricultural history. These, in turn, lead to wider geographical investigations. Indeed, the appreciation of the geography and history of a particular area should lead to an interest in its developing social history and politics — which often show through place names. Personal name and family name studies could, of course, become appropriate here, too.

Dealing with archaic, dialect, and "alien" names can help to provide the intrigue necessary to interest children in the careful study and use of words. Many place names, moreover, are deliciously poetic — Fenny Bentley, Cloebury Mortimer, Little Herbert, Sheepy Magna, Rest-and-be-Thankful, World's End...

Place names seem to feature little in schools, although they are available to all, from village to city centre. Two booklets that might be of interest, although they indicate little of the potential of names and are now a little dated, are PLACE NAMES and STREET NAMES by S & H Usherwood (1969), published by Ginn & Co. in the 'History from Familiar Things' series.

I have described a "place name game" in 'A Cheltenham Name Game', in CLASSROOM GEOGRAPHER, December 1977, Pages 22-5. The exercise is devised in the form of a "kit" which consists of (i) a copy of the town plan, (ii) a base map of the same scale, showing streams and main routes (to help orientation) and some 60 locality names — not in their present form but as their *meanings*, (iii) a checklist of the names represented, with details of their first recorded form and date, and their rootwords, (iv) a short glossary to explain the rootwords, and (v) a set of cards, each printed with one of the present-day names. The exercise is completed by placing the name-cards at appropriate places alongside the "clues" on the base map; it works quite effectively with children working in groups of half a dozen. The maps in this booklet could easily be adapted for such a "game".

Of course, name studies don't have to be parochial. Long ago, jigsaw puzzles with one county of England or country of Europe to a piece were used in teaching geography. A county or major-cities "game" might be worth developing.

Other work could centre around rescuing names. Many are now little used, because they have lost their purpose or because we have lost the habit of using them. Most field names, for instance, are known (if at all) only to older people. A study of local names of fields — or streets, or mines — could add useful material to the archives, as well as maybe generating some local interest.

Names, as we have seen, change; and some names are superseded as new ones are introduced. Youngsters often have their own (often short-lived) names for places, and these could be well worth investigating. And not only names for places. Plant and flower names have especially interesting histories (see for instance Geoffrey Grigson's ENGLISH-MAN'S FLORA, Phoenix House 1958; Paladin paperback 1975). Ideas for work based on plant names are offered in "I name this Plant", Martin Spray, CLASSROOM GEOGRAPHER, Vol. 20, Part 2, Pages 31-2, 1982.

I would be pleased to hear from any teacher who works with names — not least with plant names.

My address is — Martin Spray, GLOSCAT, Dept., of Art & Design, Oxstalls Campus, Oxstalls Lane, Gloucester. GL2 9HW.

FURTHER READING & REFERENCE SOURCES —

For <u>NAMES IN GENERAL</u> see e.g.

B. Cottle (1983) NAMES Thames & Hudson.
L. Dunkling (1974, 1983) THE GUINNESS BOOK OF NAMES
Guinness Superlatives Ltd.

SOME GLOBAL BOOKS

C.M. Matthews (1972) PLACE NAMES OF THE ENGLISH-SPEAKING WORLD Weidenfeld & Nicolson.
A. Room (1974) PLACE NAMES OF THE WORLD David & Charles.
A. Room (1979) PLACE-NAME CHANGES SINCE NINETEEN HUNDRED: A WORLD GAZETTEER Scarecrow.
G.R. Stewart (1975) NAMES ON THE GLOBE
Oxford University Press.

PLACE NAMES OF BRITAIN

W. Addison (1978) UNDERSTANDING ENGLISH PLACE-NAMES Batsford.
K. Cameron (1977) ENGLISH PLACE-NAMES Batsford.
G.J. Copley (1968) ENGLISH PLACE-NAMES AND THEIR ORIGINS David & Charles.
C.S. Davies & J. Levitt (1970) WHAT'S IN A NAME? Routledge.
E. Ekwall (4th ed. 1960) CONCISE OXFORD DICTIONARY OF ENGLISH PLACE-NAMES Oxford University Press.
E. Ekwall (1928, repr. 1968) ENGLISH RIVER NAMES.
Oxford University Press.

ENGLISH PLACE-NAME SOCIETY: Besides a specialist journal, has issued volumes for many English counties, and a dictionary of place-name elements. Some reference libraries hold copies. The introductory material in the county volumes (e.g. Cameron's volumes for Derbyshire listed below) is well worth reading.

J. Field (1971) DISCOVERING PLACE NAMES   Shire Publications.
J. Field (1972) ENGLISH FIELD NAMES: A DICTIONARY
David & Charles.
J. Field (1980) PLACE NAMES OF GREAT BRITAIN & IRELAND
David & Charles.
K. Forster (ed.) (1981) PRONOUNCING DICTIONARY OF EN-
GLISH PLACE NAMES, INCLUDING STANDARD, LOCAL
AND ARCHAIC VARIETIES   Routledge.

M. Gelling (1978) SIGNPOSTS TO THE PAST Dent.
G. Gould (1978) LOOKING AT PLACE NAMES K. Mason.
F. Johnstone (1982) PLACE NAMES 'Introducing Scotland' Series,
Spurbooks.

E. McClure (1910, repr. 1973) BRITISH PLACE-NAMES IN THEIR
HISTORICAL SETTING E.P. Publishing.
C.M. Matthews (1979) HOW PLACE NAMES BEGAN Hamlyn.
M.F. Nicholaisen (1976) SCOTTISH PLACENAMES Batsford.
M.F. Nicholaisen, M. Gelling & M. Richards (1970) THE NAMES OF
TOWNS AND CITIES IN BRITAIN Batsford.
Ordnance Survey (1973, 1981) PLACE NAMES ON MAPS OF
SCOTLAND & WALES

P.H. Reaney (1960, repr. 1969) THE ORIGIN OF ENGLISH
PLACE-NAMES Routledge.

P.H. Reaney (2nd ed. 1976) A DICTIONARY OF BRITISH SUR-
NAMES Routledge.

A. Room (1983) CONCISE DICTIONARY OF MODERN BRITISH
PLACE NAMES
IN GREAT BRITAIN & IRELAND   Oxford University Press.
A.H. Smith (1971) ENGLISH PLACE-NAME ELEMENTS (2
volumes)   English Place-Name Society.   Published by Cambridge
University Press.

H.G. Stokes (1948) ENGLISH PLACE NAMES Batsford.

DERBYSHIRE

THE MAIN SOURCE is K. Cameron (1959) THE PLACE-NAMES
OF DERBYSHIRE (3 Volumes) English Place-Name Society.
Published by Cambridge University Press.
Volume 1 covers most of the relevant area, and contains
the introduction, and sections on river and road names.

Volume 3 contains a dictionary of the name elements, and the index.

SOME OTHER ITEMS are

B. de Barri (1978) Is yours a Derby county name? DERBYSHIRE LIFE & COUNTRYSIDE January : 43-4.
I.E. Burton (1979) Place names in the Peak country. DERBYSHIRE LIFE & COUNTRYSIDE December : 72.
K. Cameron (1958) The Scandinavians in Derbyshire: the place-name evidence NOTTINGHAM MEDIAEVAL STUDIES Volume 2.
K. Cameron (1959) An early Mercian boundary in Derbyshire: the place-name evidence, in THE ANGLO-SAXONS ed. P. Cleomoes.
W. Fraser (1947) FIELD-NAMES IN SOUTH DERBYSHIRE Adland, Ipswich.
W.H. Holden (1950) A miscellany of place names JOURNAL OF THE DERBYSHIRE ARCHAEOLOGY AND NATURAL HISTORY SOCIETY Volume 23: 21-34.

W.H. Hoult (1963) What's in a name: Peakland nomenclature DERBYSHIRE COUNTRYSIDE December-January.
A. Page (1970) What is the origin of your Derbyshire surname? DERBYSHIRE LIFE & COUNTRYSIDE April: 53-5.
A. Page (1974) How some Derbyshire places got their names DERBYSHIRE LIFE & COUNTRYSIDE October: 58.
F. Vanson (1973) A POCKET DICTIONARY OF DERBYSHIRE PLACE NAMES Hub Publications, Youlgrave.

OTHER LOCAL AREAS

THE MAIN SOURCE FOR SOUTH YORKSHIRE is A.H. Smith (1961-3)   THE PLACE-NAMES OF THE WEST RIDING OF YORKSHIRE (8 volumes)

English Place-Name Society. Published by Cambridge University Press. Volume 1 covers the relevant area; Volume 7 contains the introduction, rivers, and the name elements; Volume 8 has the index.

R.W. Morris (1982) YORKSHIRE THROUGH PLACE NAMES David & Charles.
W. Thurlow (1979) YORKSHIRE PLACE-NAMES Dalesman Publications.
J.M. Dodgson (1970-1) THE PLACE-NAMES OF CHESHIRE (4 volumes)   The English Place-Name Society. Published by Cambridge University Press.

E. Ekwall (1922, repr. 1973) THE PLACE-NAMES OF LANCASHIRE E.P. Publishing.
D. Mills (1976) PLACE NAMES OF LANCASHIRE Batsford.

BOOKS BY JOHN N. MERRILL PUBLISHED BY JNM PUBLICATIONS

DAY WALK GUIDES -

SHORT CIRCULAR WALKS IN THE PEAK DISTRICT
LONG CIRCULAR WALKS IN THE PEAK DISTRICT
CIRCULAR WALKS IN WESTERN PEAKLAND
SHORT CIRCULAR WALKS IN THE STAFFORDSHIRE MOORLANDS
SHORT CIRCULAR WALKS AROUND THE TOWNS AND VILLAGES OF
THE PEAK DISTRICT
SHORT CIRCULAR WALKS AROUND MATLOCK
SHORT CIRCULAR WALKS IN THE DUKERIES
SHORT CIRCULAR WALKS IN SOUTH YORKSHIRE
SHORT CIRCULAR WALKS AROUND DERBY
SHORT CIRCULAR WALKS AROUND BAKEWELL
SHORT CIRCULAR WALKS AROUND BUXTON
SHORT CIRCULAR WALKS AROUND NOTTINGHAMSHIRE
SHORT CIRCULAR WALKS ON THE NORTHERN MOORS
40 SHORT CIRCULAR PEAK DISTRICT WALKS
SHORT CIRCULAR WALKS IN THE HOPE VALLEY

INSTRUCTION & RECORD -

HIKE TO BE FIT...STROLLING WITH JOHN
THE JOHN MERRILL WALK RECORD BOOK

CANAL WALK GUIDES -

VOL ONE — DERBYSHIRE AND NOTTINGHAMSHIRE
VOL TWO — CHESHIRE AND STAFFORDSHIRE
VOL THREE — STAFFORDSHIRE
VOL FOUR — THE CHESHIRE RING
VOL FIVE — LINCOLNSHIRE & NOTTINGHAMSHIRE
VOL SIX — SOUTH YORKSHIRE
VOL SEVEN — THE TRENT & MERSEY CANAL

DAY CHALLENGE WALKS -

JOHN MERRILL'S WHITE PEAK CHALLENGE WALK
JOHN MERRILL'S YORKSHIRE DALES CHALLENGE WALK
JOHN MERRILL'S NORTH YORKSHIRE MOORS CHALLENGE WALK
PEAK DISTRICT END TO END WALKS
THE LITTLE JOHN CHALLENGE WALK
JOHN MERRILL'S LAKELAND CHALLENGE WALK
JOHN MERRILL'S STAFFORDSHIRE MOORLAND CHALLENGE WALK
JOHN MERRILL'S DARK PEAK CHALLENGE WALK

MULTIPLE DAY WALKS -

THE RIVERS' WAY
PEAK DISTRICT HIGH LEVEL ROUTE
PEAK DISTRICT MARATHONS
THE LIMEY WAY
THE PEAKLAND WAY

COAST WALKS -

ISLE OF WIGHT COAST WALK
PEMBROKESHIRE COAST PATH
THE CLEVELAND WAY

HISTORICAL GUIDES -

DERBYSHIRE INNS
HALLS AND CASTLES OF THE PEAK DISTRICT & DERBYSHIRE
TOURING THE PEAK DISTRICT AND DERBYSHIRE BY CAR
DERBYSHIRE FOLKLORE
LOST INDUSTRIES OF DERBYSHIRE
PUNISHMENT IN DERBYSHIRE
CUSTOMS OF THE PEAK DISTRICT AND DERBYSHIRE
WINSTER — A VISITOR'S GUIDE
ARKWRIGHT OF CROMFORD
TALES FROM THE MINES by GEOFFREY CARR
PEAK DISTRICT PLACE NAMES by MARTIN SPRAY

JOHN'S MARATHON WALKS -

TURN RIGHT AT LAND'S END
WITH MUSTARD ON MY BACK
TURN RIGHT AT DEATH VALLEY
EMERALD COAST WALK

COLOUR GUIDES -

THE PEAK DISTRICT...Something to remember her by.

SKETCH BOOKS — by John Creber

NORTH STAFFORDSHIRE SKETCHBOOK

CALENDARS

1989 JOHN MERRILL PEAK DISTRICT WALK A MONTH CALENDAR